NAVEGADOR SERIES℠

Grow

Principles to create your true north

DR. ANITZA SAN MIGUEL

NAVEGADOR SERIES℠

NAVEGADOR SERIES: Grow

© Copyright 2023, Dr. Anitza San Miguel.
All rights reserved.

No portion of this book may be reproduced by mechanical, photographic or electronic process, nor may it be stored in a retrieval system, transmitted in any form or otherwise be copied for public use or private use without written permission of the copyright owner.

It is sold with the understanding that the publisher and the individual author are not engaged in the rendering of psychological, legal, accounting or other professional advice. The content and views in each chapter are the sole expression and opinion of the author and not necessarily the views of Fig Factor Media, LLC.

Cover Design by Marco Alvarez
Layout by LDG Juan Manuel Serna Rosales

Printed in the United States of America

ISBN: 978-1-959989-30-1
Library of Congress Control Number: 2023906899

Scripture quotations taken from The Holy Bible, New International Version®, NIV®. Copyright© 1973, 1978, 1984, 2011 by Biblica, Inc.®
Used by permission. All rights reserved worldwide.

I dedicate this book series to all of my spiritual mentors who have guided me throughout my life. You are all my inspiration. I have learned from each of you that without God in my life and without seeking His guidance and direction, my life would not be the same. Thank you! It is because of God's grace that I am where I am. It is because of you and your continuous support and prayers that have lifted me in my darkest moments.

NAVEGADOR SERIES℠

TABLE OF CONTENTS

Acknowledgments 5

Introduction 6

    TRUST 8

    SHINE 10

    GRATITUDE 12

    RECOGNIZE 14

    NAVIGATE 16

    FOCUS 18

    PRESENT 20

    FAITH 22

    LOVE 24

    TIME 26

    PAVE 28

    REFLECTION 30

About the Author 32

ACKNOWLEDGMENTS

A special thank you to my mentor and friend, Jacqueline Ruiz. Thank you for believing in me and seeing the "magix" within me. Thank you for helping me build my legacy.

Also, a special thank you to my husband, Juan M. Morales. Thank you for all of your support and encouragement as I navigate this journey of entrepreneurship.

Thank you to my daughter, Andrea I. Morales, for listening and understanding mommy. You are special to me and God.

NAVEGADOR SERIES℠

INTRODUCTION

When God puts an idea in my mind and heart, I listen and I take action. This book series was born of my personal and spiritual growth journey. Since the day "Navegador" was born, I knew I was embarking on a journey where my vision wasn't clear. What I have learned in the process is that time will teach me the lessons that I need to know. Time has taught me to wait on the Lord. God has not shown me exactly what I will find on my journey, but has equipped me for the journey. I am qualified for the work He has called me to do. I don't have the whole vision, but He is my guide. He is the lighthouse that illuminates my path.

My purpose is that this book, as other books in the Navegador Series, will serve you to grow the passion and potential that is inside you, so you can shine your unique light. If I did it, so can you. Everything is possible if you trust, believe, and take action.

Other books in this series are Reignite and Shine.

Blessings!

NAVEGADOR SERIES^{SM}

NAVEGADOR SERIES℠

Trust

Trust in the Lord with all your heart and lean not on your understanding; in all your ways submit to him, and he will make your paths straight." *Proverbs 3:5-6*

Trust in God in each of the areas of your life (physical, spiritual, financial, etc.). Anything that causes you anxiety, stress, tension, or worry is an opportunity for growth. Remember that in the middle of the challenge and the process you are going through, God is with you and in you. He is preparing you for something bigger and better. *Trust Him!*

NAVEGADOR SERIES^{SM}

Shine

> "Your word is a lamp for my feet, a light on my path."
> *Psalms 119:105*

Your light is unique. Let it shine. Sometimes due to life challenges and circumstances, we start to dim our light and start playing small. That was me at some point in my life. I dimmed my light to fit in. I dimmed my light because I was not confident. I dimmed my light because of impostor syndrome. As I navigate my personal and spiritual growth journey, God reminded me that I am unique and that I need to let my light shine. Are you dimming your light?

The power in His word is my guide and light. All I need to know is in His word.

Gratitude

GRATITUDE

> "Give thanks in all circumstances; for this is God's will for you in Christ Jesus." *1 Thessalonians 5:18*

As I navigate my life, I have learned that gratitude is one of the key ingredients to facing the challenges that we encounter every day. It is impossible to be negative when you are grateful.

Recognize

> "I can do all things through him who gives me strength."
> *Philippians 4:13*

When I came to a realization that I needed to admit and accept my limiting beliefs and thoughts, I discovered my true potential. I discovered that I am fully resourced to be and do what I have been created to do. I discovered that everything is possible if I trust, believe and take action.

NAVEGADOR SERIES℠

Navigate

> "You will keep in perfect peace those whose minds are steadfast, because they trust in you." *Isaiah 26:3*

We all navigate life. The question is, do you navigate in peace? Do you navigate knowing that God is in control and that He will not leave you or forsake you? Navigate in the direction of your dreams and goals. If you surrender the control, He will guide you. He will help you to navigate the unknown waters. Navigate in peace knowing, trusting, and believe that God is with you and in you at all times.

Focus

> **"**
> Set your minds on things above, not on earthly things."
> *Colossians 3:2*

We have all heard at some point, "Where your focus goes, your energy flows." Focusing on your own path, on your own journey makes the difference. I cannot compare myself to others. I have to focus on myself and my own personal growth and development.

Present

Therefore do not work about tomorrow, for tomorrow will worry about itself. Each day has enough trouble of its own." *Matthew 6:34*

Today is a gift. Navigate in the present moment. Why worry about tomorrow? Tomorrow will bring its own challenges. Unwrap the gift that has been given to you today. Every day is a new opportunity; it's present. Open it and make the best of it. You can do it!

NAVEGADOR SERIES℠

Faith

God never forgets His promises.
Keep trusting Him.
He is faithful in all seasons.

> "Because you have so little faith. Truly I tell you, if you have faith as small as a mustard seed, you can say to this mountain, 'Move from here to there,' and it will move. Nothing will be impossible for you." *Matthew 17:20*

My faith in God has been my true north, my guide. It's my superpower. When you face challenges, it is so easy to forget about your faith. Each day nurture and grow your faith. My faith in God sustains me.

Love

Carry love, carry kindness, carry grace.

And now these three remain: faith, hope and love. But the greatest of these is love." *1 Corinthians 13:13*

His unconditional love sustains me at all times. There is no greater love than the love of God. Knowing He loves me just as I am, gives me the confidence that He will always be with me. I find refuge in Him. God loves you and me. Never forget that!

NAVEGADOR SERIES℠

Time

"There is a time for everything, and a season for every activity under the heavens." *Ecclesiastes 3:1*

Time is an asset. Don't waste it on things that do not serve you. Find the time to be with yourself in connection with God. In the quiet moments, I have found the peace that surpasses all understanding. I found the guidance that I needed to navigate in the direction of my dreams. Everything has its divine time.

NAVEGADOR SERIES℠

Pave

"I will go before you and will level the mountains; I will break down gates of bronze and cut through bars of iron."
Isaiah 45:2

As you navigate your life, let God navigate with you. Let Him lead the way. He will pave the way for you. Navigate confidently, knowing that He is in control of everything. Also remember, that as you navigate, you are paving the way for others behind you. You got this!

Reflection

Let your light not shine to reflect you, but to reflect God.

As water reflects the face, so one's life reflects the heart."
Proverbs 27:19

One of the most important skills that I have developed over the last years is reflection. I have learned to stop, take a breath, and simply reflect. I have learned to shut down the distractions so that I may hear God's voice. We live busy lives. We are always on the go, but we don't take time to reflect on our day. As you reflect on your day ask yourself, "What have I learned today?"

ABOUT THE AUTHOR

Dr. Anitza San Miguel is wife, mom, scientist, educator, and transformational leadership coach. Her purpose is to help leaders reignite the potential and passion within them, so they can grow and shine their unique light, transform their mind, and unleash their potential to create their best version without limits.

Her passion for personal growth and development drives her to grow daily. She has more than twenty years of experience in research and education. She has served as a science professor and dean of science at institutions in Virginia and Florida, and currently serves as a dean leading a team in the Orlando, Florida area. She worked at the National Institutes of Health (NIH) and the United States Patent and Trademark Office (USPTO).

She is also the founder of ASM Mentors, creator of the podcast "Sacúdete y Toma Acción" translated in English as "Shake It Off and Take Action." Dr. San Miguel has been showcased in numerous platforms in social media, and other events, including TV programs in Puerto Rico. She authored *Navegador*, a reflective journaling tool with reflection cards, and was featured as an insightful author in *Today's Inspired Latina Volume X* and *Today's Inspired Leader Volume IV* book series. She is also a sought-after speaker, mentor, and coach.

Dr. San Miguel firmly believes that everything is possible if you trust, believe, and take action. Her attitude, positive energy, and determination have led her to achieve her professional and personal goals.

When she's not working, you'll find her spending quality time with her husband and fourteen-year-old daughter, traveling, and journaling.

She is passionate about education that leads to the academic and professional success of leaders with the mission of discovering their best version without limits.

DR. ANITZA SAN MIGUEL
anitza@anitzasanmiguel.com
LinkedIn: /anitza-sanmiguel
Instagram: @anitza21
anitzasanmiguel.com

To view Dr. Anitza San Miguel's other books, please visit:anitzasanmiguel.com.

NAVEGADOR SERIES℠

www.ingramcontent.com/pod-product-compliance
Lightning Source LLC
Chambersburg PA
CBHW042055050526
44107CB00110B/1171